30 THINGS MY DAD TAUGHT ME

An extraordinary book
about our dad,
your dad — and you.

IAN, PAUL AND
DENIS BAKER

First published by
Jane Curry Publishing 2011
[Wentworth Concepts Pty Ltd]
PO Box 780 Edgecliff NSW 2027 Australia
www.janecurrypublishing.com.au

Copyright © Denis Baker 2011

All rights reserved. No part of this book may be reproduced or transmitted in any form or by any means, electronic or mechanical, including photocopying, recording or by any other information storage retrieval system, without prior permission in writing from the publisher.

National Library of Australia
Cataloguing-in-Publication entry
Author: Baker, Denis
Title: Thirty things my Dad taught me/Denis Baker, Ian Baker, Paul Baker.
Edition: 1st ed.
ISBN: 978-0-9808129-8-5 (pbk.)
Subjects: Father and child. Love. Marriage. Happiness. Work.
Other Authors/Contributors: Baker, Ian James. Baker, Paul Godfrey.
Dewey Number: 306.8742

Design: Cheryl Collins Design

Printed by Jade Productions in China

30 THINGS MY DAD TAUGHT ME

IAN, PAUL AND
DENIS BAKER

This book is dedicated to our dad and to all good dads.

You show us the way and we learn from you. You love us and we love you.

We are what we are because of you.

Our dad, Leon James Baker, died on 21 February 2009.

We owned him. We loved him. He was all ours.

Not only was he our dad, but he was also a great friend, mentor and guide.

An extraordinary, ordinary man, who like so many other extraordinary, ordinary men, knew much about being a good father and husband, and perhaps more importantly about being a good person.

Our dad was married to the love of his life Dorothy, for almost sixty-six years. Dorothy was his soul mate, best friend and life partner.

We also lost our beautiful mother the same year.

Our mum, Dorothy Josephine Baker, died on 20 July 2009.

We owned her too. We loved her. She was all ours.

An extraordinary, ordinary woman of unique beauty, wit, joy and feminine grace.

Dorothy owned Leon longer than we sons, but she kindly shared the ownership with us.

Until they passed away, we managed life with the guidance and care of two wonderful people. We were blessed and honoured by the parents we were given.

We served full and lengthy apprenticeships under our parents; apprenticeships we never wanted to end.

They live on through us.

Life is too short not to make it count.

30

At the time of our father's death, I asked my brothers Ian and Paul, to think of thirty things Dad had taught them.

I added my thirty to their lists and the following pages represent a small part of the many things we learnt from our dad.

We ended up with many more than thirty things; when you are finished with the book and have written down all the things your father has taught you on the special pages, there will be many more again.

Through our dad, we learnt about being a person in our own right.

We learnt what being a father was all about.

We built our lives around what we were encouraged to believe in and trust.

We discovered much about being better people.

These are things we have never forgotten — some are little things; others hold greater importance.

Many of our thirty things may be familiar to you, and if reading what our dad taught us helps you remember what you have been taught, then cherish and practise those memories.

We all get to consider the wisdom that comes with time and life experiences.

A chance to let others know what is important to us.
A chance to reflect.

A chance to make a difference for anyone who reads these pages.

Here are the things our father taught us.

Enjoy the read.

DENIS

Our dad loved the Emerson verse below. It was written long ago, but the sentiment is not dated at all.

A framed copy of this verse sat in our parents' home — it was an expression of what our parents were all about.

These are not just words our dad liked — these are words our dad lived.

These words describe every good dad who has made a positive difference through the way he has lived.

> To laugh often and much,
> To win respect of intelligent people
> And the affection of children,
> To earn the appreciation of honest critics
> And to endure the betrayal of false friends,
> To appreciate beauty,
> To find the best in others,
> To leave the world a bit better,
> Whether by a healthy child,
> A garden patch
> Or a redeeming social condition,
> To know even one life has breathed easier
> Because you lived,
> This is to have succeeded.

Ralph Waldo Emerson
1803–1882

Everyone and everything has its place.

Never for one moment should you ever let your children doubt that you love them.

No matter what they do, or what they say, or how they may even hurt or disappoint you.

Love them.

And let them know, that no matter what, that love is unconditional.

Respect, discipline and love.

Children need to receive it.
Children need to give it.

Teach them.

Every happy, wonderful life feeds on respect, discipline and love.

You receive back tenfold what you are prepared to put in — honest work always has its rewards.

Be patient.

Take your time and the job will be done well.

You can make most things happen with patience.

Being a non-practical son, my dad taught me how to become a home handyman in all things from replacing a broken window pane, bricklaying, painting, wall papering, laying pavers and using tools properly.

I was taught much of this later in life, after I was married and had bought a home of my own.

Oh and yes, he was always there to help me with any job… and that must have taken great patience on his part, as much as it did in me learning these 'foreign skills'.

PAUL

When I was a kid of about ten or twelve, I remember fishing with my dad off rocks near a little beach on the NSW South Coast. The water was choppy and the wind was blowing into our faces, which meant that nearly every time I tried to cast my line out into deep water, it ended up closer to shore and snagged on rocks.

Snagged meant a broken line, trying to free it, lost sinker, lost hook and bait, followed by ten to fifteen minutes trying to rig the whole thing up again. Next cast, same result. I was very frustrated, very impatient, and convinced that the fishing gods all hated me.

I finally tossed the rod onto the rocks and squatted down on my haunches, dirty with the whole world. Dad never said a word, he quietly kept fishing, enjoying what really was a pretty nice day, sunny, a cool sea breeze and that beautiful blue water. He was taking it all in. I couldn't see any of it, because I was brooding in my own dark little world.

After some time my dad looked down at me and quietly asked, **'Den, what do you want to do?'**

My reply was curt and had that twelve year old tone that dripped of what a dumb question that was, **'I want to catch some fish!!'**

Dad waited a few seconds and then without looking at me said, **'You won't catch anything if your line's not in the water.'**

I sat for only a little while longer before picking up my rod and took that fifteen minutes to rig it again with sinker, hook and bait.

I never forgot that day and what my dad had said. Yep, I snagged a few more times, but I also looked around for some better spots to cast my line, I tried some different approaches, the snags weren't quite as nasty and I did catch a fish or two.

It ended up a good day. I was able to appreciate the sun, the breeze, that beautiful blue water and the company of a good mate.

DENIS

Patience and persistence will usually win out.

You won't catch anything

if your line's
not in the water.

WISDOM

Wisdom isn't found in a bottle.

It can't be bought, manufactured or made.

Wisdom grows within you.

It is fed by experience and time.

It is honed by correct actions and mistakes.

It is readily available from those who have it, and it is so often overlooked by those who don't.

Older people develop it and will share it, but we so often overlook their wisdom and lose out as a result.

The young impatiently think they have it, but they don't. It takes time.

The hurried pace of youth means that sometimes the young don't stop to listen.

My dad had wisdom; he shared it with me, I gained from it, but sometimes I overlooked it.

Dad taught me to run, to ride, to kick, to throw and to hit.

Sport is more than a game, it is an education.

Kids are designed to play games.

Kids love to play with their dads.

Dad showed me that children love adults who play games like kids.

The time available to play games with children is short.

Don't waste it.

Stand by your children but not in their way.

Dad taught me how to spin a ping-pong ball backwards with my finger,

how to juggle (badly),

and how ball bearing wheels on a billycart increased the speed of the machine.

PAUL

Try not to panic.
It achieves nothing.

Stop...
think...

and then
do what needs to be done.

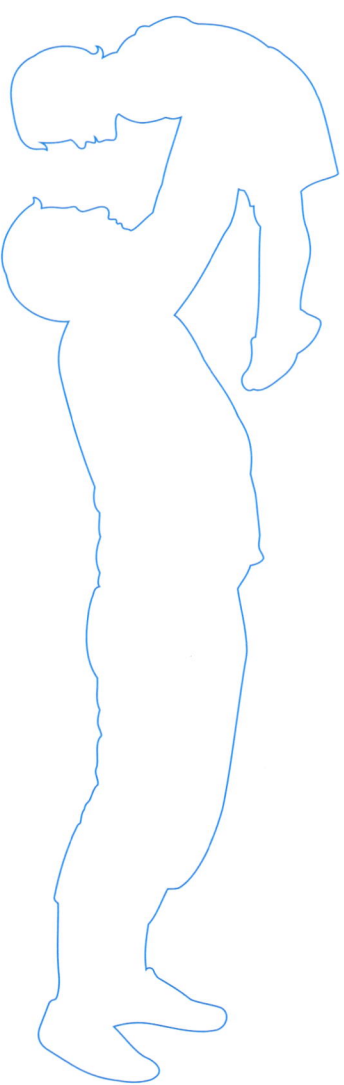

No matter what,
find reasons to

SMILE!

Show people respect if you want the same in return.

Pre-domestic sewerage days there was a time when not only your garbage was collected each week.

You also received a visit from the dunny man, who would pick up your toilet can and leave an empty one to see you through until his next visit.

Many years ago, when I was just a boy, I remember one occasion when the dunny man came to collect the toilet can. As he lifted it onto his shoulder the can slipped, the lid came off and the contents ended up all over the poor bloke.

Dad heard the commotion and quickly got him into the laundry, where dad had installed a shower. He gave the fellow soap and a towel, and while the man showered, dad washed his soiled clothes.

They ended up laughing at what had happened and together cleaned up the spilt mess.

Dad always believed no job was a low job.

Dad was also a very practical man in acknowledging the relative importance of each person. Dad appreciated how important this fellow was — because if he didn't come to pick up the can, who would?

We all have our place in life, our link in the chain — and each link is dependent on the other.

IAN

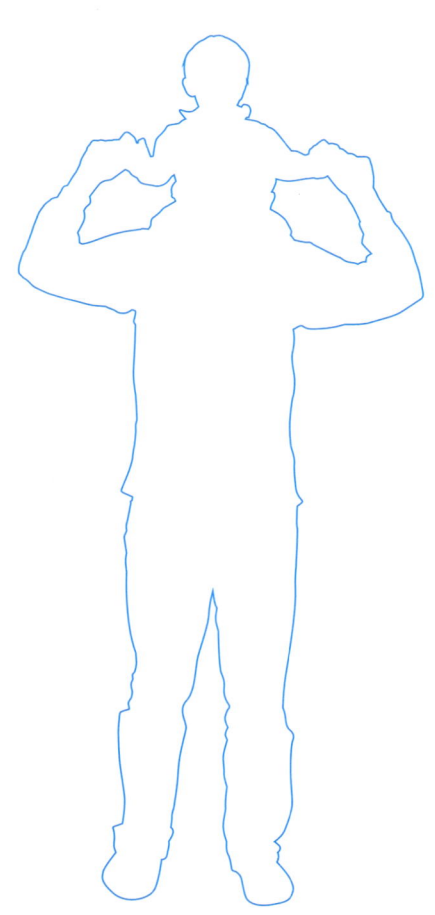

In order to respect others you must respect yourself first.

When we boys wanted something we knew we shouldn't actually get (such as an ice-cream before dinner), we would often try to get it through dad first.

Our request to dad was usually followed with his reply.

'Ask your mother.'

Which on our return from mum found dad asking,

'What did your mother say?'

As we reported the negative response from mum, dad would quickly back up mum's response with his final decision,

'No!'

We suspected dad always knew the answer to our original request, but he also knew referring to a higher authority would quickly put an end to any further demands.

Dad and his boys knew who the real boss was in our home.

Dad had a regular piece of advice
for each one of his sons, particularly
when we borrowed his tools.

'Everything has its place so
put it back where you found it.'

'If you want it to be there
next time put it back where
you found it!'

'If you're going to use that, put
it back where you found it.'

I remember one embarrassing moment when,
with my cap in hand, I asked dad if I could
borrow something to complete an urgent job.

In this case it was a soldering iron
to fix a leaky pipe.

After days if searching on dad's part,
I discovered I had it all along!

I had not returned it following an earlier job!

It only ever happened once.

Perhaps even more remarkable, he didn't
say a thing, or try to score points. He knew
I was hurting.

He knew I was saying to myself,
'Everything has a place, so put it back.'

The impact has been lifelong.

PAUL

Cure the cause not the effect.

Dad always believed that putting a Band-Aid on any problem was only a temporary measure to problem solving.

It covered the effect it didn't fix the cause.

Fix the cause and you saved on constantly replacing Band-Aids.

In most cases it is easier to fix the cause of a problem, than to be continually making repairs.

IAN

Dad always felt that if a job was worth doing, then it should be done as well as you could do it.

He wasn't fastidious about his work, but he sure didn't like things half fixed.

One frustration was a very small leak from the guttering on one side of the family house.

It only dripped in one place it shouldn't have dripped, when we copped one particularly heavy rain storm. (Not one of your regular showers of rain, or thunderstorms. It was one of those once in a blue moon rain storms that dumped huge cats and dogs.)

We could have simply placed a bucket under the leak and waited another six months before needing the bucket again.

But dad was up the ladder even before the rain stopped.

He clumped around on the roof, hung over the side, scratched around and repaired the spot he found was causing the problem.

He didn't half fix the guttering — he made sure the job was done thoroughly.

It took him some time, probably more time than was needed, but that leak was never going to win.

His persistence mirrored the need to get the job done right — the first time.

DENIS

If something
is worth doing,
do it right the
first time.

Take your
time when you
want to do
something well.

If you could only see what my dear father could do with his hands, you would have been amazed. Dad was a motor mechanic and so was I.

Dad told me that once you become a mechanic you can do almost anything.

As a mechanic you are a welder, a plumber, a fitter and turner, an electrician, a hydraulic specialist, a trimmer, a carpenter, a painter and on he would go, listing all the things, that as a mechanic, you would be faced with and have to fix. And yes, he was right.

'Now,' he would say, *'have pride in your trade and whatever it was you were doing. If it was worth doing, do it right the first time.'*

When I married and I often found myself doing repairs to my home. I sometimes took the odd short cut. Heaven help me if he had spotted my poor handiwork.

Dad's attitude about work around your home was, *'There are always things to be repaired around the home, you don't want to be doing the same repair again in the months to come. So do it right the first time and it won't need doing again for years.'*

He was so right. The average jobs I did were always needing constant repair. The well done job lasted.

Smart man my dad.

IAN

For most well done tasks, success is found in the preparation.

When I painted my house, I came to learn that

> 70% was preparation and 10% painting.
>
> Oh! The other 20%... cleaning up afterwards!

PAUL

Many, many years ago we had a cat called George.

A very easy going moggie, who was not a fighter, or a lover.

As cats go, George was highly skilled as an eater and a sleeper — a very passive, home moggie. We liked George.

A time came when a rogue, stray cat decided George's territory should change hands, and for a period of time the rogue would give poor George a terrible hiding each night.

The one-sided fights were not doing George's state of mind any good at all. So dad hatched a plan to re-establish George's dominance, dignity and domain.

George slept in the laundry at the back of house. The plan saw a string tied around the handle of the open laundry door, across the back veranda, in through Paul's bedroom window and tied around his big toe.

In the middle of the night, when the rogue entered the laundry to give George another beating, our little mate soon let us know there was an intruder in the laundry.

Paul woke, grabbed the string and a quick tug on the door captured our prey.

Here now were two cats trapped in the laundry, neither thinking about a fight (much to George's relief), both keen to get out, and dad and his sons awake and ready to put stage two of the plan into action.

Suffice to say, a hessian bag, four human males, two uncertain pussy cats, an hour of stalking and wrestling with one increasingly angry cat and multiple scratches and bites suffered by the human hunters, finally found George safely in our arms and the rogue wrapped in the bag with only its head sticking out.

The next stage of the plan found Dad holding the rogue, while one of his boys was holding George in an unfamiliar boxing pose in front of the bagged pussy cat.

No harm was planned for either cat, and no harm eventuated.

Here we were at 3am, trying to re-establish George's manly confidence.

In a blur of fur, claws and flying paws, suddenly both cats broke free and escaped from the laundry.

But instead of heading in different directions, to escape one another, the fleeing felines ran side by side down the driveway, out through the front gate and up the road.

George returned after a while. His desire for food always outweighed any other fears.

So at 3.30am, a father, his three sons and one heroic cat called George shared a very early morning breakfast.

We saw the rogue a few times after that, but he never returned to George's laundry, he never bothered our little mate ever again.

George still specialised in eating and sleeping, but he took on an air of confidence that was measured by a new found arrogant walk.

The plan worked! So did the Dettol and bandages that helped repair all the scratch marks and wounds we suffered.

He was a good cat, our George.

It was a good plan, Dad.

DENIS

There is often more than one way to successfully do most things.

THIRTY THINGS MY DAD TAUGHT ME

So what has your father taught you? Here's a place to write those thoughts when they enter your head.

Appreciate the
good times.

Loyalty builds friendships and cements trust.

Dad always backed us.

He always was, and still is, by our side.

Loyalty was one of Dad's greatest traits.

After the war Dad went to work as a motor mechanic for a local Chevrolet car dealer who later on became one of the oldest Holden dealers in New South Wales.

This association was to last thirty-five and a half years.

There were many times during this period when Dad was asked to work for other dealers, but Dad's loyalty was such that he remained true to his employer till the day he retired.

Dad explained to me his reasons for staying, and the insight I gained from him was to benefit me throughout my working life.

Times have changed and loyalty in the workplace may not be what it used to be. But it is not dead — nor should it be.

Loyal, respecting relationships between employer and employee can be the cornerstone of good business.

IAN

 Think before you act.

Children need reliable oldies.

Always be there for them.

In the good times...
and even more so, when your children are in trouble.

**'Be tolerant.'
With the people
you love.**

**And even with
people who may
not deserve it.**

Dad worked as a long-term Service Manager of a GMH dealership.

One thing that always amused my father was the attitude of people when it came to their motor vehicles.

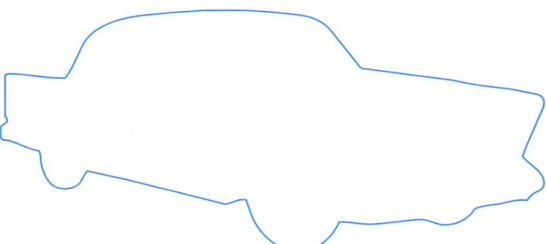

The degree of tolerance he would show was amazing; he would allow the customer all the time in the world to get whatever it was off his chest, never interrupting and then in a calm but firm manner he would endeavour to solve the problem.

I remember one day a customer had expressed his anger with a problem he was experiencing, that to him wasn't being diagnosed quickly enough.

The customer had just driven his car up to the workshop, hopped out of the car, walked to the counter and in pouring out his problem, abruptly demanded, 'What's the cause of the problem? I want it fixed now.'

The car needed to be checked over before a diagnosis was possible, but he wanted it fixed on the spot.

Eventually the problem was located, fixed and the customer was eventually on his way.

Dad looked at me and said, 'I should have been a doctor. A patient will sit for hours in a surgery waiting to see the doctor and when he eventually does, he will accept the delay and then all the running around to specialist services, until all the information is collected, to then allow the doctor to diagnose the patient's problem.

But we as mechanics have to instantly know what the problem is and have it fixed before he gets out of the car.'

IAN

On one other occasion, many years ago, Dad was confronted by a very angry and very aggressive man, who having recently purchased a brand new (manual gearbox-column gear lever-three speed) car was returning for the second time with a faulty gearbox.

He was incensed about the poor quality of the car and the apparently previous failure of Dad and his mechanics to fix the problem. He threatened he was one step short of exposing the manufacturer, the dealership, the service department and Dad personally, to every national newspaper, television and radio station in the country.

The car was checked and yes, there was a problem with the gearbox.

A day of servicing the car, and replacing the gearbox, saw Dad drive a long distance to the customer's home to personally deliver the car that night.

The customer was still on his high horse when Dad arrived.

The car had purred like the proverbial cat on the way over to the customer's house, so Dad invited him to take it for a drive with Dad as his passenger.

The car started, no sign of noise, or any possible problem.

The customer then pulled the car straight into third gear and released the clutch.

The car duly bucked and jerked before stalling.
The customer screamed at Dad – that nothing had changed – the car was a lemon!

My tolerant Dad then spent a further hour providing a driving lesson for the customer, who until that time had been unaware the car (or any other car) had a 1st and 2nd gear (as well as 3rd and reverse)!

Even then, Dad lost the customer from that day, probably too embarrassed to show his face for any return service.

IAN

Forgive people.
We are all capable of making mistakes.

Don't stew over things.

It only works to let little problems become much bigger than they should.

Talk things over.

Listen — and then — work things out.

BE A GOOD NEIGHBOUR.

Dad's philosophy.

For most of us, it is more than likely that we will have the same neighbours for a fair length of time.

Some will come and go, but there will be those who will be there long term.

They will be a large part of your life.

They will need your help and you in turn will need theirs.

They will share in your joys and in your sadness.

They will borrow your tools and sometimes forget to return them (well, until you give them a subtle reminder).

They'll be there when you need a shoulder to lean on and an ear to chew on, and they'll look after your home when you're away.

If you are a good neighbour your neighbour will be good to you.

IAN

Honesty will keep good people by your side.

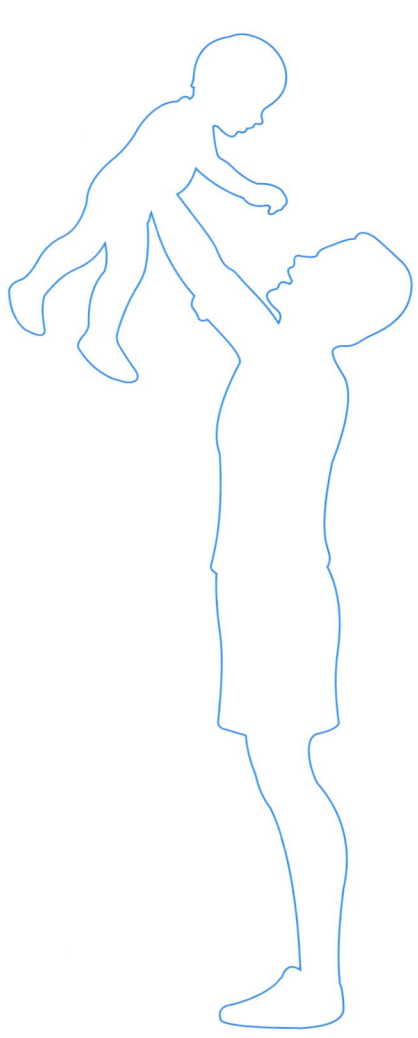

The most valuable gifts you can give someone you love, don't come with a price tag, or fancy wrapping paper.

Lead by example.

Don't ever cheat.
With anything, or with anyone.
Be strong in your faith.

Whatever your belief may be.

Dad was a convert to the Catholic religion.

A commitment he made prior to marrying Mum and a commitment that he never wavered from for his entire life.

I have no doubt that he found strength from his faith and that this faith guided him in all that he did.

Days prior to Dad's passing the local parish priest called around to see how Dad was doing in the hospital, where Dad had been staying for several months.

After that visit Dad had a beautiful calmness and an acceptance in the way he looked, and in the way he would talk to us.

Dad told us that he was ready for whatever happened.

His faith gave him peace.

Dad (and Mum) both believed there were two commandments (before you ever concerned yourself with the Ten Commandments).

Honour your God and
Honour your neighbour.

They felt if you could manage those two points the rest would pretty much look after themselves.

Be responsible for your own decisions and actions.

Discipline.

Children need it.

Adults need to apply it to their children and themselves.

For it to be successfully applied, it doesn't need to be accompanied with loud words or a slap.

Be involved in your children's lives.

Give children your time.

Even if you don't have much time to spare.

Make the time.

They need your time and you need to provide it.

Take nothing for granted.
Appreciate what you have.

There are always two sides to a story, take the time to listen, understand and consider them both.

> (This was one of Dad's greatest attributes, he would always size up the situation, take time to think about the possible outcomes and make a fair and firm decision.)

Z Z Z Z Z Z Z Z Z Z

**Always sleep
on big decisions.**

Z Z Z Z Z Z Z Z Z Z

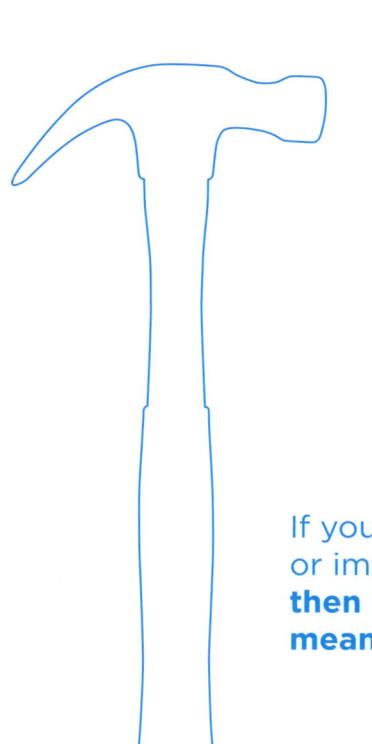

If you're going to use a tool or implement of some kind, **then learn how it is meant to be used.**

Be yourself.

I spent many years with my father. We fished together, we worked together, we shared joy and pain together; we had similar ideas and we respected each other's differences; we built things together and we tore things down together.

I saw the pride and excitement in his eyes when I completed my apprenticeship and my final exam achievements. I saw the same pride when my brothers saw their achievements realised.

The same again when his grandchildren were born and an even greater excitement when his great grandchildren came along.

I saw the great love he had for his wife, my mother, and that was evident right to his last breath.

Even though he may not have known or realised, these were lessons in life he taught me.

He also taught me what was right and what was wrong and how to live a good life.

I learnt these things by just being with him, listening to him and watching him.

He taught me to be myself.

I was always able to hug and kiss my father and found it the easiest and most natural thing to do, even when I was older and a father myself.

I have asked myself on a number of occasions since Dad's passing, 'Will I miss him?'

I do miss him, but his presence will be with me always and what he has taught me will continue to guide me for the remainder of my life.

Dad, what you taught me, I have taught and passed on to my children. My remarkable father lives on.

IAN

Nil Desperandum

(Let there be no despair)

Thank God for husbands and little boys.

(Was Dad's counter to extreme anti-male views!)

But for grandfathers and fathers, babies wouldn't be possible.

(Always said tongue-in-cheek. No man respected or appreciated women more than our dad.)

'Don't dabble in what you don't know.'

'Stick to your expertise and know your limits.'

'Learn more about what you don't know.'

I was 18 years old and had started work.

Influenced by others I followed a horse over nine race meetings (I was told it was a certainty each time). I lost more than I could really afford each time.

Come the tenth race I didn't back it. It won!

You get the picture on 'expertise' and 'limits'. Dad knew about the bets, but he said nothing more than above.

His message was thunderous.

It was the reason I never took up gambling.

(Of course the stock market is not really gambling…is it?)

PAUL

Don't gamble any more than you can afford to lose.

If it sounds too good to be true...it probably is!

You will always know when the time is right

...there is a little voice inside of you which will let you know.

THIRTY THINGS I'D LIKE TO TEACH OTHERS

(Here Dad are pages for you to add things you have learnt over time, things that are important to you, even things your own father may have taught you. These are your pages.)

One kind action can make a big difference in people's lives.

Close to fifty years ago Mum and Dad met a couple, Bill and Agnes, who had recently migrated to Australia from Great Britain.

Their first home was a small caravan, in a low rent caravan park in western Sydney.

Without any request, Mum and Dad supplied their new friends with blankets, clothing and kitchen implements along with other things, that helped them settle into their new world.

Dad also provided a reference to help Bill secure his first job.

Bill and Agnes deserved support; Mum and Dad knew they were good people, and our oldies found the action a very simple step to take, even though Mum and Dad were low income battlers themselves.

Fifty years passed. Bill and Agnes worked hard, built a home, raised a family and positively touched many other people through their lives.

Fifty years passed and the love and respect found between true friends never faltered.

Bill and Agnes were there at Mum and Dad's funerals. True friends who shed a tear with us and stood with us to support us.

All four lives were enriched through simple acts of kindness.

Never in their lifetime did Mum and Dad ever have finer friends.

IAN, PAUL & DENIS

Judge a person by what they do, not by what they say they are going to do.

You finish first when you are prepared to put yourself second.

This was Dad's very simple philosophy, when it came to being a husband, a father and a friend.

Sometimes there are things that just have to be done.

**Tough decisions.
Problems to be faced.
Issues dealt with.**

Consider those issues, decide on the best possible actions, and keep yourself together, for as long as you need to get it done!

Dad often said,

'I could not have chosen a better time to live, than in my lifetime and with what I have been so privileged to enjoy.

Science and medical discoveries.

Advancements in flight and space travel.

And knowledge.

I have lived through a wonderful time in man's existence.'

Life can either be a game or a war.

No one really ever loses in a game, there are never any winners in a war.

Dad never saw any sense in wars, fighting or hurting people. He strongly believed wars achieved nothing. Consequently he rarely, if ever, spoke about his role in World War II. He displayed open anguish at the folly of men in any conflict.

> Dad was a pacifist, who would reluctantly become a hero when needed.
>
> In his entire life, he never hit anyone.
>
> But there were odd times, when knowing what was right, he did stand up and face an aggressor — in support of his family, friends and workmates.
>
> He did what was right and dealt with aggression with assertive action and reconciliation.
>
> As a result he never had cause to ever hit anyone.
>
> His belief was that wars (and fights) didn't decide who was right, only who was left.

Anger is negative energy.

If you are not in control of yourself, then walk away until you are.

The easiest example of this was shown when Dad was driving the family car.

On the occasions some mug was tailgating our car — that driver being a real hoon on the road — Dad would simply pull over and let him pass.

The hoon would pass and within a few minutes he was both out of sight and out of mind.

It worked every time.

Do you remember how certain things saddened and horrified you as a child?

Remember because they are probably things that still make you sad and horrified now.

I have recalled many times my horror as a seven year old at a husband known to our family who openly beat his wife.

I had inadvertently heard Mum and Dad discussing this late one night when I should have been asleep.

Dad said to me, 'Remember how you feel now and carry it with you for life.'

Physical harm to women is totally unacceptable in my value system. Indeed harm of any description.

PAUL

Little things do make a big difference.

He taught me that simple pleasures provide the sweetest memories.

As a child things like camping, fishing, kicking a ball, a holiday walk along a beach at nightfall, taking the time to talk and listen to his son.

As an adult things like happy times with friends and relatives around a dinner table, gardening, fixing things, a cup of tea, letting me take Mum and him for a drive, and taking the time to talk and listen to his son.

DENIS

Times may change but the ability for children to find their way into strife never seems to go away.

I well remember my Dad bringing home borrowed golf clubs for his, once a year, business golf day.

I also remember that our backyard looked bigger than it really was.

Outside the back fence of our quarter acre block sat a very impressive glasshouse, part of a large garden and plant nursery.

How could I forget the best three iron shot I ever hit, then or now, as it sailed over the fence and met two large glass panels at speed.

With the nearest golf course several kilometres away, I had little defence when the nurseryman visited Dad that afternoon.

Dad soon taught me about two stroke penalties for being out of bounds.

Still, it was a great shot...

DENIS

Friendship, respect and love are earned by parents — not bought or raised through fear.

Worrying is
a waste of time.

Worrying about something will not make it any better.

Most of what we worry about never happens anyway.

THIRTY THINGS MY DAD TAUGHT ME

(What has your father taught you? Here's a place to write it down. You don't have to do it all at once — just when those thoughts enter your head.)

Be responsible for
your own actions.

If you know you shouldn't do it — don't do it!

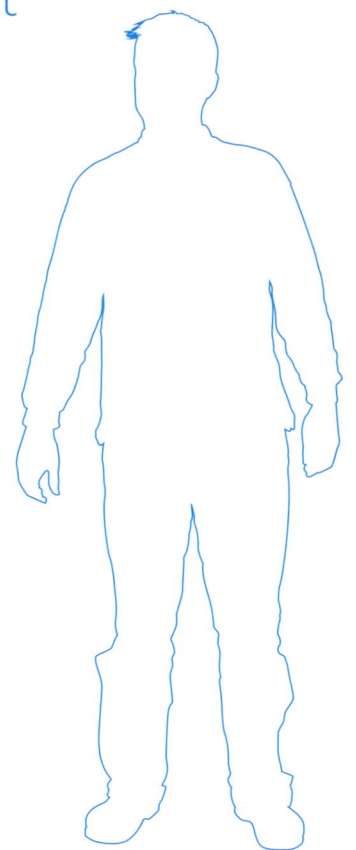

It's not easy to say no.

But strong people know when to say no.

Weak people give in to the easier option.

Try to make a difference in your world.

Dad taught me to share.

Dad always liked the crusty slice of bread on each end of the loaf.

So did I.

But without a word being spoken between us, I always let him have the crusty slices on the ends of the loaf.

I always liked chewing on the bone of a baked leg of lamb.

So did Dad.

But without a word being spoken between us, he always let me have the bone of a baked leg of lamb to chew on.

DENIS

Value good friends and **treasure their company.**

Take pride in your work.

Dad was a wood turner after he retired.

His beautiful bowls and timber stands were never sold. They were given away.

Many, many pieces of his wood turning craft are found in the homes of family friends and relatives.

It was never enough to simply turn out a bowl and quickly paint it with lacquer.

Every piece was turned, shaped, reviewed, sanded, reviewed, painted, reviewed, sanded, painted, reviewed, sanded, painted and reviewed until it had reached a finish that he felt was worthy of being given to someone to put in his or her home.

In no way was it a vanity thing. Dad simply took great pride in what he did and how his finished work reflected his skill and care.

I guess if you take the time to make something, or do something that reflects who you are, you do have every reason to take pride in your efforts.

DENIS

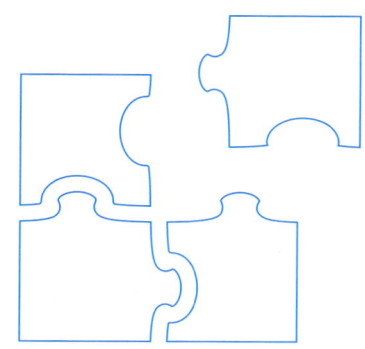

Dad believed we were all put on this earth for a reason.

How we lived our lives and how we impacted on others was in our own hands.

He believed that life was meant to be enjoyed.

He believed we should value ourselves and work at making our lives and the lives of people we touch positive and happy.

Care about people.

Dad told me that as long
as I had done my research,
to make sure that
**what I thought was right,
actually was right,**

**it was then that I
should stand up for what
I believed to be true.**

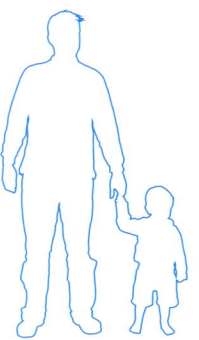

He taught me to love without demands or conditions.

My dad was a very easy man to love.

It was the love held between father and son, the love that exists between best friends and the love that simply came through mutual respect.

I loved the fact he was always reliable. You knew about his morals and beliefs — and they never wavered.

He would consider alternate points of view, and he was strong enough to change his mind, but his core beliefs never wavered.

You knew he would listen to you, even when he was busy.

He knew when you had problems, even before you had opened your mouth.

He would either have an answer straight away, or he would think about the matters and get back to you (usually that day, or at worst the next morning).

He felt your pain when things were not right. He didn't just feel it, he would grab your pain, and take a big chunk of it to carry himself, so your load wasn't as heavy.

He was a happy man, who appreciated simple pleasures like ice-cream, a freshly mowed lawn, a hearty dinner and good friends.

He was so easy to love.

DENIS

Our dad loved our mother with passion.

You knew it, you saw it, you felt it.

Real love.

Mum always came first. She was always treated with the upmost respect.

Dad conveyed to us that our mum was a woman, a beautiful lady and a person in her own right.

And as with all women she was to be treated with the greatest respect.

Dad had his moments of great frustration. Those times when man and woman just don't seem to make sense to one another. But his underlying respect for Mum never wavered.

They occasionally argued, and they might have raised voices, but he never once yelled at, or belittled, our mother in any way.

AND, they always seemed to settle the difference before they went to bed that night.

Dad did give his life to Mum and she in turn lived for him and loved him just as much. All built so much on mutual respect.

The last three months of our dad's life saw him in hospital for all but one or two days.

Our beautiful mother was suffering from progressing dementia. Something that had been developing over the previous two or three years.

Dad and Mum still lived in the family home — a home that had been a very happy and very safe place for a long time.

Dad, his sons, close friends and relatives all knew of our mum's condition.

When Dad entered hospital, we had reached a stage where reality was simply demanding care for Mum that was only possible in a professional aged care environment.

It was so hard to deal with — so hard to imagine life without our father and mother in the family home.

Dad was a sick man. He had a major operation within a very short period of entering hospital and at the same time, he was also diagnosed with inoperable cancer. He had only a very short time left.

With Dad's blessings we boys battled through paperwork, heartache, disappointments and very real moments of despair, as we tried to find a safe and dignified place for Mum to enjoy her remaining life in peace and care.

Dad knew every step of what was going on — we were working as a team to find the right pathway to care for Mum.

The very day we had seemingly exhausted all possible avenues, we discovered a beautiful respite care place for Mum. It came out of the blue (but it was built very much on prayers, research, phone calls, letters and the particular persistence of big brother, Ian).

On a Wednesday in February Mum, with her boys by her side, found a new home in a beautiful dementia care hostel.

The following day, we sat with Dad and let him know the lady he loved was in dignified care.

Dad expressed his relief that Mum was okay and reassured his three sons that he loved us, he trusted us and was so thankful for what we had done.

Forty-eight hours later our Dad died. As you so often hear, he simply let go, once he knew his bride was safe.

Now that really is love. Never ending love. Mum certainly knew how to pick a good bloke.

DENIS

Enjoy every minute of every day.

Those minutes and days can never come back again.

So don't waste them.

Dad showed me that a good father will always be there for you,

particularly when you are scared,

or lonely,

or when you have worries that you just can't seem to beat.

You don't have to hit
someone to hurt them.

Choose your words thoughtfully.

Making things is great for the body and mind.

Make the most of what God gave you.

Never hate anyone.

Hate is too strong a word to use on another human being.

The energy of hate will wear you down more than the person you direct it at.

**Save for the future,
it will come along soon enough.**

Adults are not infallible.

It's okay to be human in front of your children.

It's okay to occasionally be wrong.

It's okay to say sorry.

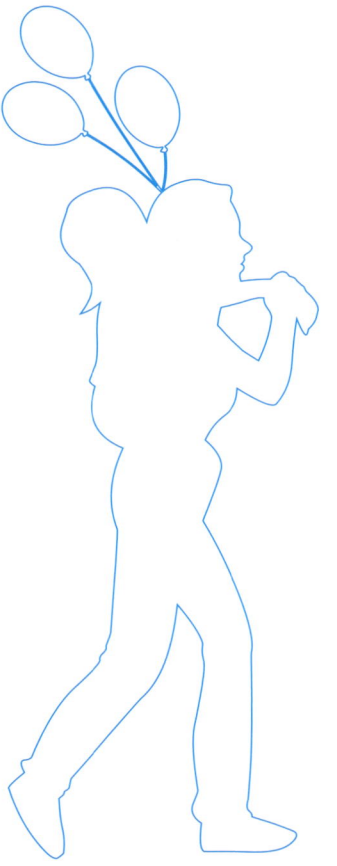

You're allowed to make mistakes.

You're allowed to cry.

You're simply a human being human.

A broken vase is just a broken vase.

The person who gave it to you is important, not the pieces on the floor.

THIRTY THINGS I'D LIKE TO TEACH OTHERS

(Here Dad are pages for you to add things you have learnt over time, things that are important to you, even things your own father may have taught you. These are your pages.)

Don't be so serious about everything.

It really is never too late to be whatever you want to be.

Never give up.

Never.

For if you quit, that will be the very moment a door is about to open.

You can do it.

Put your mind to something and you really can do it.

Nothing is that bad that you can't overcome it.

The sun always comes up tomorrow.

Laugh and encourage others to laugh with you.

One of Dad's favourite stories related to the fact that our mum looked after all of their finances. This was an arrangement that suited both Mum and Dad, and never once caused any bother or strife between them.

Our very hard working Dad would hand over his unopened weekly pay packet to Mum each Friday, ceremonially kissing the envelope goodbye.

In later years, very much tongue-in-cheek, Dad would tell people that Mum only ever gave him 50c a week pocket money.

He claimed he once asked for an extra 50c a week and Mum accused him of keeping another woman!

Dad would laugh and Mum would feign shock at his claim.

(The story about the 50c was not true in any way; I'm sure Mum only ever gave him 20c a week pocket money, the same as we boys received.)

DENIS

Time really does heal pain.

(And so do people you love and trust.)

In his latter years, suffering
from growing illness and pain,
Dad would often tell me,

'Don't grow old mate.'

Until the day I told him
I didn't like the alternative.
He smiled at me and said,

'Okay, you can grow old,

but do your best to stay well.'

DENIS

For each one of us,

There is nothing so badly broken, that it can't be fixed.

There is no problem so big, that it can't be remedied.

There is nothing you have done, that can't be forgiven.

There is no hurt, that can't be healed.

As long as we want it.

Your children will learn more from your actions than your words.

In your life, particularly your work life, seize opportunities and shake them for all they are worth.

Don't doubt yourself.

You are better than you think.

Every child needs a pet.

Pets help children learn about life and death.
A cared for pet will always be a good friend.

Having been certain of something, so certain you would vigorously argue the point, only to then discover what you thought was, in fact, wasn't, is the perfect time to smile, **apologise and calmly move on.**

Dad, almost ten months to the day since you died, five months to the day since Mum died, we have just signed the paperwork to sell the family home.

Your home.

And yes, it does touch me as I write these words, because I am feeling one of those times when I really am missing you.

This is one of those times that just sneak up on me, as I remember moments I spent with you. As I remember your actions, the tone of your voice, your face, your walk. There are these times when I so much wish you were still here.

I do miss you Dad and it does hurt not having you around.

Your absence heightens how good it was to have a dad like you.

The sale of this house, that was your home, and Mum's home, and my home, and the home of each member of our family, is a time of now letting go.

This is certainly not letting go of fine memories and fine times, but it's about letting you and Mum go, so that we can move on.

The house was a home that you built. Not just a home of bricks and cement, but a home filled with spirit.

Your spirit.

I miss you Dad, because you gave me reason to miss you.

I love you Dad, because you gave me reason to love you.

There is no end to things.
What appears to be an end,

                is in fact, always
                a new beginning.

'I wasn't there that morning, when my father passed away. I didn't get to tell him, all the things I had to say.'

The Living Years by Mike and the Mechanics

As I was driving back to my home after my brother's phone call to say Dad had passed away, the song *The Living Years* was playing on the radio and this particular verse stuck in my mind.

Here I was 130kms away and I never had the chance to say my final goodbye to my father. I still think about it even now but what would I have said if I had the time over and I was able to say, 'Bye, Dad.'

He knew that he had prepared me for this time, in all that a loving father does during the years of raising his children and what he had taught them — faith in your Creator; the life's skills that he had passed on; knowing right from wrong; respect for your fellow man; the unquestioned love for a wife and mother; the eternal love for his children and forgiveness of a son's mistakes; the creation of a strong and unbreakable bond that a father shares with his children.

I loved him and he knew it and neither time or distance made any difference. I really didn't need to be there, there really wasn't any more I could have said that he already didn't know.

I believe that Dad knew that it was his time. He had completed all the tasks that the Lord required of him and that he being the husband, father and person that he was, left us satisfied in the knowledge that he had done the best he could.

From a loving son, Dad you did better than your best, you did great.

A huge part of you Dad is in me and I can't thank you enough. My only wish is that I achieve being half the person you were.

IAN

My 91 year old father's last discussion with the doctor in hospital included a simple request.

**'Get me the hell out of here!'
Such was his desire to live.**

**'I love you and tell Mum I love her.'
These were his last words to us before embarking on the greatest journey of all.**

I saw in Dad a spirit — a noble and generous spirit that understood compassion, revelled in achieving, fed on laughter and treasured family.

A spirit that knew courage, humility, fair play, truthfulness and honesty to the highest degree.

He was the consummate person to have by your side in any situation. Indeed the more grave the situation – the greater the danger – the better he was.

His was a great spirit. He was my hero.
My adviser and my best friend.

Dad, while I may miss you, your spirit stays — it lives on in the values you displayed.

From you we draw our strength.
You will always be with us.

We celebrate your life and I thank you for being my dad.

PAUL

From the time I was a young boy I dreaded the day my father would no longer be around.

If he was late home from work, I'd be camped out at the front gate waiting for him to come home. In later times if he was late getting back from the shops or a doctor's appointment, I would be on edge until I knew he was safely home.

In very recent years, when I stayed overnight at the family home, I would find myself checking on both Mum and Dad when they were asleep, just making sure I could see them breathing.

When Dad passed away, after his prolonged illness, we had been through several months of preparing for his final day. When it came, it was more surreal than real.

He was such a good dad. So much my good mate. A man I truly loved.

The memories will not fade. I think of him every single day.

I talk to him when I need advice, and each time I talk to him, I hear what he has taught me. And therein lies my strongest understanding of my dad and what can make any dad special.

That although my dad is physically gone, he is still here with me in everything I do, everything I say, in every thought I have — my father taught me to be who I am.

I am a reflection of my father.

And I am very happy and very proud to be my father's son.

DENIS

Dorothy Josephine Mitchell was born on 11 March 1917. Mum grew up in NSW at Richmond and later Earlwood.

She was an accomplished pianist and singer, and studied at the Sydney Conservatorium of Music. Mum was the eldest of five children (growing up with four younger brothers).

Mum and Dad had a deep love which grew stronger over almost 66 years of married life.

They had what science refers to as a symbiotic relationship.

Two people who shared one life and one love
for each other.

THE BOYS

IAN

Ian and his wonderful wife Denise raised four children and have four beautiful grandchildren.

Now retired, Ian has achieved much in a lifetime career as an automotive technician.

He has also been a very active community worker, particularly involving young people and sport, and the care and support of elderly and infirm people in our community.

Ian loves fishing, lawn bowls and the Sydney Swans footy team.

PAUL

Paul and his wonderful wife Mary raised two children and have four beautiful grandchildren.

Paul worked in very senior levels of both public and private sectors of the education, employment and training industries.

He was very involved in community support, and provided help for people living on the streets of western Sydney.

Paul was keen on flying and all sports, and like both his brothers, he was a very good cricketer and footy player in his younger years.

DENIS

Denis is the single son, who in jest would often blame Dad for advising him to stay a single man. That of course always drew one of those well known wifely glances from Mum.

Denis has worked in both the public and private sectors of the education, employment and training industries.

Denis is a writer, trainer, newspaper columnist and public speaker.

He loves sport and has written several books related to employment and sporting topics.

IN MEMORY OF OUR DEAR BROTHER PAUL

Our brother Paul died just weeks after we finished putting this book together.

Paul died too young, after a year long battle with cancer. He was only 61 years old.

He was a good brother and a good mate.

We're sure Paul is right now enjoying a heavenly cup of tea with Mum and Dad. *('The first cup out of the teapot — no sugar — one chunk of chocolate cake please'.)*

His love for our parents is reflected in every page of this book.

Paul's great love for his partner in life, Mary, his children and his grandchildren was always unwavering.

He loved being a dad and he was darn good at it.

A wonderful man — a wonderful father — just like his dad.

We love you brother.

And we miss you so much more.

ONE FINAL THOUGHT

Every dad is unique in his own way.
Unique in the quirks of his words and actions.

And so it should be.

What we have written about our dad, what you have written, and will write about your dad, what dads write about their dads, will help us each remember and honour what it is about dads that makes them so special.

There is no life without a dad.

In these pages we have found a reason to smile, to reflect and remember at least thirty things our dads have taught us.